HOW TO COPE WHEN YOU ARE SURROUNDED BY IDIOTS...

OR IF YOU ARE ONE.

■■■■■■■■■

By Wayne Allred

Illustrated By David Mecham

■■■

Published by:
Willow Tree Book
P.O. Box 640
Roy, Utah
84067-0640

ISBN 1-885027-03-6

First Edition published in 1993.
Second Edition with additions published in 1994.
Third Edition published in 1995.
Fourth Edition published in 1996.
Fifth Edition published in 1997.

Designed by David Mecham
Printed in the United States of America

TO THE STUDENTS OF ROYAL HIGH SCHOOL, WHO CONTRIBUTED TO THIS BOOK MORE THAN THEY WILL EVER KNOW.

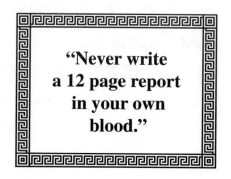

"Never write
a 12 page report
in your own
blood."

W.A.

CONTENTS

Idiot: (*s. dimus witus*)

A feebleminded person who hasn't the good sense that God Gave Broccoli.

THERE IS NO NEED FOR ALARM, BUT IDIOTS ARE TAKING OVER THE PLANET

Do you often feel that you are surrounded by idiots? To me they seem to be everywhere. They are in my office, on the job, attempting to wait on me, in the classroom, even in my home. In fact, it is entirely possible that you, the person who is attempting to read this book right now, could even be a complete idiot.

What can be the real tragedy about this deluge of bumbling incompetence is that many people who are incredibly stupid and terminally obnoxious don't even realize

1

it! Do you know how annoying it is when people who don't know how dumb they are try to act smart?

Even if you, yourself, are not totally inundated with idiots like I am, I'm sure you at least know someone who has idiotic tendencies. Until now, there was simply nothing that you could do about it. Most idiots were stuck bumbling around and doing embarrassing things forever while the rest of us were forced to try to either avoid them, or just tolerate their stupidity.

But now, finally, relief is in sight. This monumental work can train you, your pathetic friends, children, employees, or students in 101 of the most important and fundamental skills that are essential to getting along in life as an idiot. If you can manage to master the information taught in this course, even if you are pretty darned dense, some people might be fooled into thinking that you're normal and, short of that, you might at least confuse some of the rest of the people concerning the extent of your stupidity.

WHERE DID ALL OF THESE IMBECILES COME FROM?

Some of my readers may not even be aware that this inundation with bumbling incompetence and stupidity is a fairly recent phenomenon. Things weren't always this bad. Why, just a few short years ago, there were so few idiots that just to find one was unusual. Each town only had one or two so-called "village idiots" and everyone knew who they were. Many even had their own business cards. Idiots were a scarce commodity, something special.

This is no longer the case. Our world has changed dramatically in recent years. And it is these important changes which have caused this sharp increase in stupidity.

In order to be able to find solutions to this dilemma, we first need to have a thorough understanding of the source of the problem.

And so, if we're looking for the biggest problem first, only an idiot could over look

3

politics. Abraham Lincoln, or somebody once said, "Power corrupts and politicians never give a sucker an even break. . . or something." How else do you explain the fact that perfectly normal people, once they get elected to some office, begin to forget everything: from who they hired, to who they gave instructions concerning millions of dollars of drug money, to who they have slept with, and, what they promised to do if elected?

And don't just sit there and say, "tsk, tsk, tsk." "I don't happen to be a politician and so politics aren't making me stupid." If you are saying this, not only do you have serious speech problems but you are a real ditz. This is like saying "if I fall head first into a septic tank, it won't bother me that I forgot to floss my teeth." Because of the fact that politicians are constantly before you in the media and on TV, you are having what remains of your brain numbed daily by your contact with them.

Of course there are other causes too, such as drugs, environmental pollution, exposure to MTV, being hit by cars, eating nuclear waste, smashing beer cans against your head, being a city person, having your lips run over by a train, and being named Barney, but by now I'm sure you get the point that idiots have increased to alarming numbers.

There is one more cause that we must consider individually here and that is the "family" problem, the problem of idiots raising idiots.

The traditional nuclear family, with a mother and father and 2.8 children, is gone. In its place are families with 1.8 parents, families with two or more parents holding down 3.8 jobs per parent who are probably on drugs, families with cats, families whose homes were built on toxic waste dumps, families who never watched E.T., families who drank a quart of paint thinner thinking it was Vodka during the last trimester of each pregnancy, and families with 4.8 latch-key children working 2.8 jobs in order to post bail for their one parent who probably abused them while they were on drugs. If

5

you have a family like one of these, not only do you have a legitimate reason to be an idiot, but you could make some big money on Geraldo or Oprah.

THE OFTEN UNRECOGNIZED BURDEN OF STUPIDITY ON SOCIETY

I am certain that we have missed some of the causes, but the important point is that public education and the employer have been called upon to deal with these problems. And I'm ashamed to admit that I have done a very poor job. This heavy burden upon the backs of teachers and employers has become a major impediment to progress, especially since so many of these mutant students and workers grow up without the common sense God usually grants an average squid. All seriousness aside, for those of us in business and education the terms: "he doesn't have the brains that God gave broccoli," or "she

7

doesn't have the sense to come in out of a nuclear winter," are all too familiar and often literally true. Too many students and workers are completely baffled by problems like whether or not to eat a live cockroach if there's $5.00 in it, whether they should try to get their busy boss's attention by using a spinning table saw blade to flip a large bolt and bop him on the head, or whether or not to reach down into the bad part of an outhouse to retrieve a quarter that they dropped...and some other pretty basic things that they really should know long before they have to deal with a teacher or employer.

Having personally been in both business and education, I finally reached the point where I was fed up with having to deal with idiots. And so I spent at least a year's worth of "banking" holidays and in-service days, exploring ways to remedy the problems of students arriving at school, or of employees arriving at work, so lacking in good judgment that sane people wondered how anything could be so obnoxious and still be allowed to live. My research has provided the solutions that can help students, children, employees and other bumbling idiots in all walks of life deal with their condition.

To begin with, let's take a look at two steps which, if taken, can eliminate a lifetime of frustration and embarrassment for those who are "functionally brain-dead", or who have the more easily treatable form of the problem which professionals have now labeled "common sense disadvantaged." We normal people just call people like this "idiots."

STEPS TO TREATMENT OF THE PROBLEM OF STUPIDITY

The first step in the treatment process is for educators or employers to administer an exam for all enrolling students or prospective workers which covers some of the most essential life skills and knowledge. This booklet contains an exam designed to do just that.

Then, after having identified without a doubt who are the true complete idiots, they are in a position to simply refuse to admit each of the confirmed idiots into the classroom or into the workplace. Those

11

persons would then be sent home where their parents could spend some more time working with them and getting them more ready for real life.

STEP 2

I can sense that some of you are already getting ahead of me here. You have identified the obvious flaw in this program. I admit that many of these people really don't have the brains that God often gives to a pretty average stand of broccoli and since the source of their intelligence genes were their parents, how can you expect parental idiots to train idiotic children? You can imagine what happens when you get people with the brains of common rest room algae attempting to teach their offspring, who have the brains of very small rest room algae, how to function in life.

It looks like we have put our finger on a major problem here. Step 1 all by itself simply won't work because, in most cases, more parental support is so out of the question. We absolutely must include step number 2, and have the schools and business community teach these parents and their children a remedial course in essential life skills. Call it "Bone Head Common Sense", if you will; it's the only humane thing that we can do. This very book has been written as the syllabus to this course. It can help business leaders train common sense disadvantaged employees. It can help teachers teach important life skills to dense students, and it can teach fully functional parents step by step, exactly how to prepare their potentially normal kids to be qualified to enter the classroom or, for that matter, the parking lot. And, as explained above, it would probably be a good idea if some of the parents took the course right along with their children.

Because idiocy is so common, and because some who are dense are too stupid to know it, we have prepared this test to help you to first, determine if YOU are an idiot, second, determine if those around you are dense, and third, gauge the degree of seriousness of the stupidity in question.

THE STANDARD CALIFORNIA IDIOCY EXAM

PART 1: MULTIPLE CHOICE

1. When people around you need to get your attention, do they usually:

A. Quietly and humbly call you "Sir", "Madame", or "Your Highness"

B. Yell "YO!" as loud as they can, and then your name

C. Whack you between the eyes with a 2X4 or some other large piece of building material

2. What is the most important thing that you do each day with your head?

A. Develop solutions to unique and complex problems which have plagued mankind since the beginning of time

B. Try to keep from screwing things up at work or school

C. Pound nails and smash empty beer cans

3. When you have a few hours of free time do you choose to:

A. Read Shakespeare, Tolstoy, Wayne Allred, or Emerson while listening to Wagner or Tchaikovsky on your quad stereo

B. Watch Gilligan's Island reruns on TV. while belching between swigs of beer and bites of pizza

C. Cling to a rock as plankton-rich seawater flows through your palate

PART 2: TRUE-FALSE

4. Cats can swim just fine while relaxing inside a gunny sack in the canal.

5. The best source of accurate news is in supermarket tabloids.

6. The Pope is Catholic.

7. Your Senator, Governor, or Representative will make a sincere attempt to keep all of his or her campaign promises after they are elected and also will scrupulously follow all ethics and campaign laws.

8. Snakes have Armpits.

9. The best way to get rid of hiccups is to swallow the hind quarters of a Cape Buffalo intact.

10. Chickens definitely have attractive lips.

ANSWER KEY

1-**3**. As with all multiple choice questions, there is no "technically correct" answer, these are all a matter of opinion.

4. True, many people are not aware that most house cats actually prefer to sleep inside a damp gunny sack while resting in the canal.

5. True, the flip-side of this is that often times information from news sources that appear credible, like the evening news or your newspaper, can be dangerously misleading.

6. We can't be sure. The only thing about The Pope that we can be certain of is that because he is a white adult male he is sexist and a bigot.

7. Right, and your pet gerbil might cough up the Hope Diamond.

8. True, but only during the larva stage.

9. True, this works every time.

10. True, but you probably won't have much luck kissing them either.

HOW TO SCORE:

Give yourself 15 bonus points if you did not bother to actually take this test. If you took this test, regardless what grade you got, if you are not a complete idiot, you are probably at least an imbecile and should consider getting remedial help for your condition by signing up for one of the wonderful weekend seminars that we hold regularly at the resort beaches in Yakutsk.

If you took this test, as described above and can begin to accept the fact that you are a confirmed idiot and want to know the extent of your stupidity, score 2 points for each "A" answer on questions number 1 through 3, and 1 point for each correct answer on True False. Then, have someone put their finger on top of your head while you twirl around and around. (Just kidding

19

of course, many college professors use this technique to help relax before taking a test.) Then follow closely the instructions on how to determine your grade.

GRADE AS FOLLOWS:

If you scored 15 or higher, good news! You probably have only slightly below average intelligence.

12-15: You are most likely a Dork, or at least, you're not too quick and if you want to appear normal, you should definitely not hang out with quick-witted people.

9-11: You are probably considered by those people who you thought were your friends to be a ditz.

5-8: You are a geek and a definite embarrassment to your family.

2-4: You are a confirmed drooling,

stumbling, bumbling, and the butt of all the jokes idiot. Avoid contact with anyone you don't want to embarrass.

If you scored below 2, If you are alive, you are definitely a lower life form, probably a mollusk.

(THE FIRST EVER)
HOW TO COPE
WITH IDIOTS
TRAINING
COURSE IN
BASIC LIFE
COMPETENCY

Now that you know whether or not you are an idiot, it's time to do something about it. Let's use this course to help you or to aid in training the idiots who surround you in some important life skills.

It's best if those who are NOT idiots do the teaching. We cannot accept responsibility for results if a confirmed idiot teaches this remedial competency course.

In an effort to avoid unduly burdening or stressing anyone, We have included here only the first 101 lessons, those that cover the things that you should absolutely never do. There are many more lessons we could add, such as not floating face-down in the septic tank, or not applying your own tattoo with a wood burner and latex house paint, but these subjects are probably material for a post-graduate level intelligence course. Absolutely do not attempt to comprehend these higher level concepts until you have completely mastered the more basic skills in this booklet.

HOW TO TEACH THIS COURSE

In order to use this booklet effectively, read and follow these instructions carefully:

First, If you are not an idiot, assemble the entire group of confirmed idiots who you want to teach together in a room. Have them sit comfortably, but far enough apart so as not be a danger of hurting each other.

Next, since so many of these students are probably not auditory, kinesthetic or, for that matter, visual learners, which means that they are only capable of learning when pain is involved, systematically demonstrate each lesson using the students as examples. For instance, lesson number one has to do with the proper use of machinery such as a blender. The best way to teach this lesson is to bring in an actual working blender, leaving something very tasty stuck to the bottom. Get one of the densest certified idiots in the class to be your helper and have him or her attempt to lick the bottom of the blender. Just at the precise moment when his or her tongue is licking the bottom...plug it in. This should provide a vivid object lesson which will clearly make your point about lesson number 1, at least as far as your helper is concerned.

After this demonstration simply go to lesson number 2, and demonstrate it in much the same way, then demonstrate numbers 3, 4, and so forth.

Third, follow up will be required.

National tests on average students, children, and employees show that the length of the memory of the typical high school student is something less than 4 nanoseconds, unless you are talking about the rules to a video game or a steamy part of an "R" rated movie. And since the high school students that were tested have substantially longer memories than YOUR employees, students, friends, or children, you will need to reinforce the principles that you teach very often. As regularly as 20 or 30 times per day, you should choose one or more of these lessons that needs to be reviewed and while casually walking past the student, yell the lesson at the top of your lungs. Example: (This is most effective if you can catch the student in the act of violating the rule...) Yell loudly something like: **"Don't try to disarm dangerous explosives while hung over."** Scientific studies have shown that the louder you can yell, the longer they will remember.

If you follow this procedure exactly, I think that you will be amazed at how quickly these students will pick up this essential information.

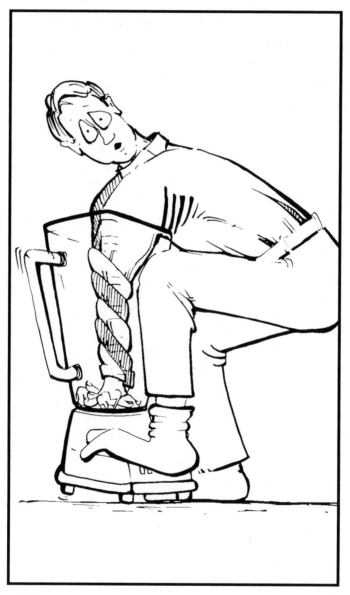

THE LESSONS: 101 THINGS THAT YOU SHOULD ABSOLUTELY, POSITIVELY, UNQUESTIONABLY NEVER DO

Lesson #1

You should never ever attempt to lick the bottom of the blender while the blades are still turning.

Lesson #2

You should absolutely never drink a quart of vinegar after first having eaten a box of baking soda.

29

Lesson #3

You should never store your pet turtles, gerbils, and rabbits in the gas tank of your father's car.

Lesson #4

You should never attempt to drive a large nail into hardwood using a banana as a hammer.

Lesson #5

You should never lean your metal step ladder against high voltage wires or large turbines.

Lesson #6

Don't encourage Alligators to eat small fish out of your hand.

Lesson #7

You should never attempt to clean up nitro-glycerin or nuclear waste with a vacuum cleaner.

Lesson #8

Never use your children as collateral for a loan.

Lesson #9

Never attempt heart bypass surgery or major angioplasty on others without proper training; or on yourself without adequate supervision.

Lesson #10

Never store small pets or children in a microwave oven.

Lesson #11

Never slide down a sandstone rock formation naked.

Lesson #12

Never get in the way of a herd of Sumo wrestler's on their way to dinner.

Lesson #13

Never keep large snakes in the same pen with baby chickens.

Lesson #14

Never ever remove dried, raw egg or bird poop from the paint job of your new BMW with a pocket knife or razor blade.

Lesson #15

Never attempt to trim your fingernails with a chain saw.

Lesson #16

Never allow someone to hit you on the head with a baseball bat unless you're wearing a good helmet.

Lesson #17

Never pinch the pimples on a gorilla's face.

Lesson #18

Never poke pets smaller than a tadpole into your nose.

Lesson #19

Never drive west in the east bound lane of traffic on the freeway.

Lesson #20

Never vomit on your mother's nice furniture.

Lesson #21

Never go skinny dipping in a septic tank.

Lesson #22

Never stick your finger in a moving fan just to see what happens.

Lesson #23

Don't pitch your tent on the beach down near the water at low tide.

Lesson #24

Never attempt to change your flat tire without first moving your car out of the fast lane of the freeway.

Lesson #25

Never put your sleeping bag in the tall grass near a swamp.

Lesson #26

Never ever tie your dog to the landing gear of a commercial air liner.

Lesson #27

Never look up when sea gulls are over head.

Lesson #28

Never spit into a fan.

Lesson #29

Never attempt to adjust your TV antenna during a lightning storm.

Lesson #30

Never play golf in the snow using a white ball.

Lesson #31

Never allow anyone to shoot an apple off of your head with a bazooka.

34

Lesson #32

Never eat yellow snow.

Lesson #33

Never lick your fingers immediately after picking your nose.

Lesson #34

Never go swimming wearing white shorts and no underwear.

Lesson #35

Never smoke while siphoning gasoline.

Lesson #36

Never close a serious abdominal wound with a spot-welder

Lesson #37

Never eat salt while sucking on a slug.

Lesson #38

Never microwave dynamite.

36

Lesson #39

Don't put poisonous spiders, scorpions, and ants in your swimming suit.

Lesson #40

Never kiss a cobra

Lesson #40.5

Never pet a porcupine.

Lesson #41

Never drive a convertible through an automatic car wash.

Lesson #42

Never rub your eyes after handling hot sauce, peppers or onions.

Lesson #43

Never slide down a banister that has razor blades in it.

Lesson #44

Never look down the barrel of a loaded gun.

Lesson #45

Never staple someone's lips together.

Lesson #46

Never ever die with dirty underwear on.

Lesson #47

Don't attempt to drive a 24 foot high truck under a 20 foot bridge.

Lesson #48

Never try to trim your nasal hairs with a weed eater.

Lesson #49

You shouldn't open your mouth while riding past a beehive.

Lesson #50

Never detonate nuclear weapons with a match.

Lesson #51

Don't ever go water skiing when you have diarrhea.

Lesson #52

Never sit on a toilet seat immediately after it has been cleaned with hydrochloric acid.

Lesson #53

You should never go to school or work without first getting dressed.

Lesson #54

Never play mud football in a tar pit.

Lesson #55

Never eat a T-Bone steak in front of a Doberman pincer.

Lesson #56

Don't water ski behind an inter-continental ballistic missile.

Lesson #57

Never clean a Picasso or Van Gogh with Clorox.

Lesson #58

Never attempt to teach your pit bull to lick your face.

Lesson #59

Never eat fuzzy, green cheese or meat.

Lesson #60

Never substitute poison ivy or stinging nettle for toilet paper.

Lesson #61

Never dry your hair with a blow torch.

Lesson #62

Never pick your scabs while swimming with sharks.

Lesson #63

Never buy a solar powered flashlight.

Lesson #64

Never light fireworks after playing with gasoline.

Lesson #65

Never eat green pudding made by a person with a bad cold.

Lesson #66

Never blow-dry your hair while taking a shower.

Lesson #67

Never hold onto a propeller after the boat starts moving.

Lesson #68

Never eat in excess of 200 lbs. of steel ball bearings immediately before swimming.

Lesson #69

Never try to write a 12 page report with your own blood.

Lesson #70

Never attempt to clear up your complexion by burning off your zits with a blow torch.

Lesson #71

Never use the bottom stall of a two story out house.

Lesson #72

Never attempt to adjust the lawn mower blade while it is turned on.

Lesson #73

Never finger paint with super glue.

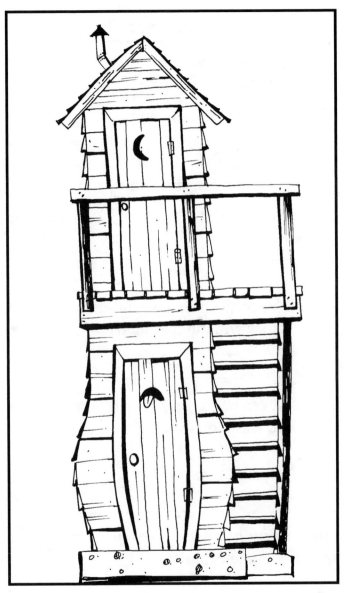

43

Lesson #74

Never chew your gum without first removing the tin foil.

Lesson #75

Never attempt to milk a wolverine.

Lesson #76

Never hunt pheasants with nuclear weapons.

Lesson #77

Never sleep in a septic drain field in wet weather without a ground cloth.

Lesson #78

Never build your dream home on top of a toxic waste dump.

Lesson #79

Never fly a loaded passenger plane upside down while an *Airport* movie is showing in the cabin.

Lesson #80

Never drive at speeds greater than the posted speed limit...squared.

Lesson #81

Don't ever try to expose your black cousin from Zimbabwe to American culture by bringing him to a Klan rally.

Lesson #82

Never attempt to embalm one of your friends while he's sleeping... just as a practical joke.

Lesson #83

Never go hang gliding in a hurricane.

Lesson #84

Never enter a butt kicking contest if you have only one leg.

Lesson #85

Don't attempt to find re-usable toys and valuable antiques by straining them out of the city sewer with your shirt.

Lesson #86

Don't make noises like a wounded antelope while sneaking through the lion's cage.

Lesson #87

Don't chum for alligators using live politicians.

Lesson #88

Don't attempt to operate an industrial sewing machine while sniffing glue.

Lesson #89

Don't suck on the tailpipe of a pickup truck while the engine is running.

Lesson #90

Never use a jackhammer to dislodge popcorn hulls from between your teeth.

Lesson #91

Don't throw footballs, baseballs, or Frisbees in an incubator.

Lesson #92

Don't accept a massage from someone who is using a power sander.

Lesson #93

Never feed your mink by placing chunks of their food on your tongue.

Lesson #94

Don't clean your ears with a power drill.

Lesson #95

Never ever try to mow the grass in a mine field.

Lesson #96

Don't brush your teeth with a horse biscuit.

Lesson #97

Never examine a person's nose while they are sneezing.

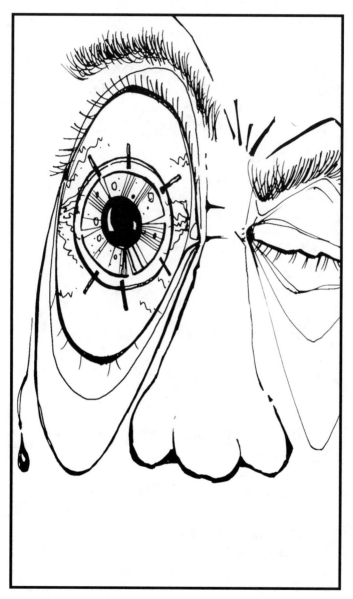

48

Lesson #98

Don't put your contact lenses in with a stapler.

Lesson #99

Never attempt to tip the highway patrolman who pulls you over for speeding.

Lesson #100

Never eat oysters, sauerkraut, rutabaga, *and* sweet and sour liver casserole two days in a row.

Lesson #101

Don't allow your friends to inflate you with hydrogen just so you can see what it would be like to fly

6 OUR DREAM

While we do have our work cut out for us, the dream of "every idiot a harmless idiot" is within reach. We promise that if you find yourself surrounded with idiots, or if you are one, if you will apply the principles taught in this course, interesting things will happen.

It may not be easy for some of you, but try to imagine for a moment what life would be like if you never had to listen to stupid questions. How would your life be better if everyone in your group got the punch line of your jokes without any further explanation. Imagine your peace of mind if you knew that you could leave the workplace and your subordinates were capable of limiting, somewhat, the damage that could be caused in your absence. And finally, visualize how proud you would be if you had an outside chance of not being embarrassed by one of your offspring when you went out in public.

I'm sure that no crummy course, especially one that only costs a couple of bucks in a book like this could ever do all of that, but we have to make outlandish claims like that to get you to buy it, and besides...we have to start somewhere, we have to do something about all of these obnoxious idiots, even if it's wrong... and this book is definitely something.

Begin teaching today, and let's make this world a more tolerable place. We could start a major movement and our slogan could be "Idiot Free in 2003!", or "A Harmless Idiot is the Best Idiot", or "An Idiot is a Terrible Thing to Waste Your Time On", or "Give a Hoot be Astute", or "Give

52

Me an Above Average I.Q. or Give Me a Job that Isn't in Fast Food", or or "Ask not What You Can Do for Your Country, Ask How your Country Can Get Rid of all these Idiots!"

AN IMPORTANT EXAMPLE OF GOVERNMENT RELATED IDIOCY

I want to make it perfectly clear that I am not paranoid, but it seems to me that we Americans have an idiot-related crisis on our hands. I.R.S. agents are everywhere! They are in our homes. They are in our offices. I'm pretty sure that last night I saw one peeping through my kitchen window. It's amazing that I am not paranoid, because I found evidence the other day that they had been out sifting through my compost pile. Some days I have seen them behind the car seat, under

55

the refrigerator, at the office, in movie theaters, and behind the shower curtain. All paranoia aside, I could swear that I even saw one the other day who was actually using my old golf clubs.

On any given non-holiday, my house is almost completely full of thousands of faithful public servants who are trying their darndest to help me sort out the confusion about some of my assets that I have received bad information about. I am deeply grateful for their efforts. It turns out that there have been quite a few things that I thought were mine, and that I had actually planned to use, which now belong to the federal government. Can you imagine my embarrassment?

This work that these agents are doing is an important public service, and while I deeply appreciate it, I have to admit that having so many of them around at times can get a little irritating. Many of them have their hand out, and I don't think that I'm being paranoid when I observe that some of them have been known to actually try to take some of my stuff without even asking.

Personally, I don't have as much of a problem with this as some people because I'm not at all paranoid, and besides, I'm pretty much used to this kind of abuse. I am married and have teenage children. But for many Americans, the constant pressure being applied by this vast army of dedicated public servants is the most stressful issue that they must deal with in their lives; and they are not happy campers. It is primarily for the benefit of these people, and to show that I am clearly not paranoid, that I have written this chapter.

For those of you who don't know me, I am a civic-minded, patriotic individual who is definitely not paranoid. Not long ago I wanted to do something to help my country and so late one evening, after I had finished scraping my important financial documents off from the bottom of the bird cage and re-assembling them so I would be ready for my daily series of I.R.S. audits, I took some time out and went to work on this problem. I wanted to see if I could dig up some information about why there seem to me, a typical non-paranoid American citizen, to be so many I.R.S. agents. My research led me to discover some alarming things. But, since some of the things I found out, if misunderstood, could harm innocent people (namely me if something in this book should accidentally offend or irritate any of these I.R.S. agents) we need to proceed cautiously by first taking a look at what I believe to be the heart of the issue.

THE HEART OF THE ISSUE

Lest any one misunderstand me, I discovered that the problem is not that the I.R.S. agents aren't fine people, and it's not that they aren't performing an important and worthwhile service. The problem is simply that there are in fact upwards of three hundred times as many competent, dedicated, and conscientious agents attempting to collect taxes as there currently are actual tax payers. Amazingly, after painstaking research, and at great personal expense, I was able to pinpoint the precise federal agency where this problem of so many agents began. I was also able to come up with an ingenious solution to the problem which I will describe in some detail later in this work. As a matter of fact, I uncovered a small human error that had occurred in an obscure office in an oval-shaped room in The White House, which for a brief moment caused the federal hiring mechanism to go berserk.

If you are to understand this book and my proposed solution to the problem properly and if my solution to the problem along with my contention that I am not paranoid is to receive any credibility, you need to be given a little background about this research.

THE RESEARCH

In the beginning, as we began to search for clues about why the government has so many agents, it seemed logical to start in the personnel office, since this was basically a personnel issue. So we started looking for clues in the Federal Office of Personnel (**F.O.P.**). Little did we know at the time that our quest for information would take us on a trail through literally millions, if not billions, of government departments, some familiar to most Americans, and some obscure. In our research, we were required at great personal risk to pass through scandals, cover-ups, plots, depredations, hokey sales presentations, tasteless jokes, schemes, murders, trite, over-used cliches, intrigues, death, and violence, not to mention non-designer clothing and poor color coordination.

Having run into this much resistance simply by going to the local post office to mail an odd-sized package, we knew that we must be on to something big. We felt that this could be a scandal the size of Watergate, The Iran Contra Affair, President Clinton's underwear, or even President Reagan's former Polyps. Regardless of the costs or risks, we now knew that we must

60

press on for this was a story that demanded to be told. This trail of the hiring glitch led up through the Federal Urinal Development Department (**F.U.D.D.**), and then through the **E.P.A**. (The department of Elevated Payroll Advocates). It was here that an anonymous tipster who called himself "Deep Doo Doo" referred us to the Army, and then The Navy, and then the Marines, and even to the Congressional Resource Allocation Panel (**C.R.A.P.**). Next, we found a lead that took us to the Department of "Senatorial Legal Experts who give Assistance and eaZe Embarrassment" (**S.L.E.A.Z.E.**). where we followed the trail to the office of Major Useful Congressional Outside Unidentifiable Sources (**M.U.-C.O.U.S.**), Department of Unnoticeable Getaways for those of High-level (**D.O.U.G.H**.), The Government Research And Fact Finding Task force (**G.R.A.F.F.T**.), The Bureau of Un-reformed Retired Politicians (**B.U.R.P.**), and finally to the Federal Agency of Retired Toasters (**F.A.R.T.**).

And so, on a very limited budget ($1.00 borrowed), and in roughly the time it takes a typical person to complete the removal of their own gall bladder with a sharp rock and their teeth, skateboard across the Gobi Desert, or stand in line for a passport, we completed the research and solved the mystery surrounding this vitally important subject.

Having followed this trail to its conclusion, to our great surprise, we found that it ended at the very pinnacle of power, the precise spot where high powered decisions effecting the lives of every man, woman, and child on the face of the planet are made, where the very future prospects of life as we know it hang in the balance.

From the office of the Wife Of the President (**W.O.P**.), we went over to the Federal Department of Dungeons and Official Pain and Torture (**F.D.D.O.P.A.T**.), where experimental pain tolerance research is conducted, and where human beings are drawn and quartered (next door to I.R.S. headquarters). And then they sent us to the

Office Of the President himSelf (**O.O.P.S.**), who, according to official government protocol, was blamed for the actual problem. It was there, naked to our very eyes, that real life government insiders revealed some juicy gossip, great rumors, fascinating speculation, and the official version of the truth about what happened, and this is it:

₿ 10,178,421

₿ 10,178,422

₿ 10,178,423

₿ 10,178,424

₿ 10,178,425

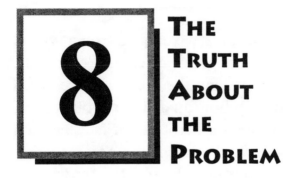

THE TRUTH ABOUT THE PROBLEM

We found out that one afternoon the Federal Department of Personnel of the United States of America received and was conned into promptly filling a bogus order to hire 25,000,000 people.

"How could such a thing have happened?" you ask. "Don't we have a government filled with multiple checks and balances, Senators, Governors, Congress-persons, and Geraldo Rivera?" The truth is simple, but disturbing, and you taxpayers who are now dealing with the problem have a right to know exactly what happened.

HOW THIS HAPPENED

You see, a few years ago, on a typical day in Washington, former President, Reagan was having the secret service touch up his hair when an Iraqi secret agent, disguised as Ross Perot but in fact, bent on creating havoc within our government, delivered a proposed executive order that clearly asked the president to create an additional 25 million Revenue Agency jobs.

President Reagan, with his hearing aid turned down, and in Nancy's absence, misunderstood the part that said "create an additional 25 million revenue agency jobs" and naturally thought his aid was saying, "mate those miserable 25 million humane society dogs." Since this seemed like a decent and politically correct thing to do because most of the dogs were going to be put to sleep the next day, and it seemed kind

and gentle enough to let them go out of this life with smiles on their faces, without a moment's hesitation, President Reagan signed the bill into law.

Next, Congress, who could have blocked the bill because there was on that day a quorum of 3 members present since their junket to Monte Carlo had been canceled as a result of the fact that all of the ring-side seats to the Mike Tyson/Sylvester Stallone fight had been bought by talk show hosts who have more influence, were sitting in the corner of the hall playing blackjack and rolling dice for stretch limousines and sexual favors from each other's secretarial pools. Since Senator Graftworth from Illinois was on a roll, they naturally weren't able to stop right then just to consider a bill that didn't directly concern a Congressional pay raise. And so without opposition, the bill passed into law.

All congress persons were immediately wired the good news and encouraged to return home from their vacation resort research projects to lobby in order to insure that their individual constituencies received their fair share of the allocation of jobs. Thanks to the modern-day miracle of the fax machine, it then took over 40 minutes to fill those 25,000,000 high paying civil service positions.

WE HAVE A PROBLEM

I guess when all is said and done, it really doesn't matter how we got all of these extra federal workers. The simple fact is that we have them, and that creates a major dilemma: If we lay all of these people off, even though it would substantially reduce the federal deficit, stimulate our economy so that we would pay off the national debt in 2 years, free up billions of dollars to fund such social programs as health care for everyone, and providing free condoms in all of our elementary schools, and because it would effectively double the average national per capita standard of living, we would have a major problem for politicians

69

who would then be forced to grapple with the issue of how to find new jobs for these 25 million people.

While this might seem like a reasonable enough trade-off to all of you mis-guided, uninformed or politically incorrect typical working persons who have thousands of dollars of excess money that you're pleased to use to pay the taxes that support the federal programs and keep people fed and clothed, and support the charities which really help the poor, and to take care of their own kids and families, and who only use government programs as a last resort, and who do their civic duty,... it would create a major rebellion among the majority of voting Americans.

The problem then is; If we don't lay off all of these excess workers, or we don't find something else to do with them, there might not be any actual working tax PAYERS left outside of jail, gainfully employed. I know that I personally won't be able to afford to provide copies of my tax return for all 25,000,000 of these guys all by myself and the other taxpayer is busy right now working on his last appeal before they send him up the river. No, something really must be done about this problem of too many agents.

PROPOSED GOVERNMENT SOLUTIONS

Even though it is truly the "American way," we may not be able to let the Federal Government solve this problem for us. Although they have been trying, and even though they would like to solve it when it comes to this particular problem, for some reason they just keep coming up with bogus solutions.

For starters, they tried using all these extra agents to give advice and help taxpayers who had questions about their tax returns. However, this network of helpers never got in sync with the actual tax laws.

73

A tax payer's chances of getting the correct answer from them was statistically only slightly better than his chances of having a meteor made of mayonnaise hit him on the head, wining the $70 million lottery and having a living, breathing, non-mechanized human being at the bank, all on the same day.

Since those were unacceptable odds, they went on to try plan "B" which was to have them keep busy by attempting to install a new highly sophisticated income tax auditing super computer every 2 years, but this didn't work either. They kept ending up with computer systems that were good at tearing the arms and legs off from delinquent tax payers and twisting them into interesting origami designs, but they were no good at all at sorting out tax problems from the millions of returns that were submitted. (Now that I think of it, I'm probably not sure that I want them to ever master this capability because if they do, the government will know things like: how many days we wear the same underwear, and that we hate oysters, and that you hide

$20.00 under the salami in the refrigerator, and have an obsession with Ninja Turtle movies and young sheep.)

Now, in desperation, they're talking about using these millions of agents to collect delinquent student loans, government insured mortgage payments, casino gambling debts, and to enforce inner-city gang territorial claims. While we know that they are perfectly capable of doing these things, to have agents of our federal government do them does raise some serious and deeply disturbing ethical questions such as: should a delinquent taxpayer have the right to bleed on carpet in what was previously his home, but which is now property of the I.R.S?; and with all of the adult males now in debtor's prison, is it proper for women under the age of 6 to fill dangerous combat roles?; and when a jailed taxpayer has had all of his finger bones broken during interrogation, is it legal for a 3rd party to dial the number of his one allowed phone call? No. These issues are much too complex, and therefore make this option too controversial.

"OBJECTIONABLE MATERIALS
INTERCEPTOR"

10 THE REAL SOLUTION

It is true that we have a big problem on our hands. However, as bleak as things look at the moment, there is a glimmer of hope. As it is with most problems, it's solution will depend upon Yankee ingenuity; upon the average guy on the street. Since there are still two of us figuratively, but not quite yet literally on the street and, since one of us, me, has an actual solution, I humbly submit this study to Congress in a spirit of pure patriotism, without any self-interest, or for that matter, paranoia, as a concerned citizen of the United States of America.

A BOLD SOLUTION TO THE PROBLEM OF TOO MANY AGENTS OF THE I.R.S.:

We can find things for them to do other than attempting to find and collect taxes. Now, I know that at first glance, to most of our political leaders and those working within the government, this may sound like an extremely complex, if not completely incomprehensible solution to the problem. So, in order to help them understand, I'm going to type very slowly. Also, to keep the cost of the study and implementation of this plan as simple as possible, I have done all of the approximately 45 minutes of research myself, and I am providing step by step instructions on exactly how this job re-structuring can be done. I have provided a list of 55 different things that can be done with this army of "excess" I.R.S. agents, and I have broken this list down into categories so that the job titles can easily be written by even the slowest government employee. I do have one final word of caution.

78

A WORD OF CAUTION

While most of these proposed jobs are quite simple. Some are extremely useful and practical. While we have made every effort to eliminate such jobs, a few may have slipped through. You may feel free to ignore any of these. Before proceeding consult competent legal counsel. Void where prohibited by law.

ONE ADDED NOTE

For bureaucratic convenience, I have included useful titles and acronyms along with some of these job descriptions in order to aid government officials in their negotiations with the union representatives of these "excess" agents and to make the transition to other types of jobs smoother. To ask a federal official to go from say, "Divisional Head of Collections" to something like "Laundry Bag" would make this proposed package pretty difficult to sell.

55 USES FOR I.R.S. AGENTS

CATEGORY 1.
CIVIL SERVICE JOBS

$$$$$$$$$$$$$$$$$$$$$$$$

They could be used by the forest service and environmental researchers as bait to catch certain endangered species like polar bears and crocodiles. We could talk them into accepting the change by offering them an important sounding job title such As: "Endangered Species Acquisition Facilitator".

They could be used by "Super Fund"

81

for difficult environmental cleanup projects which require skills such as cleaning toxic waste by hand. Their job title could be: "Special Director of Chemical Re-stabilization".

$$$

Because of their familiarity with tense situations and their skill under pressure, they could be used by law enforcement officials in very volatile cases to do things like break up domestic disputes.

$$$

One of the many "natural" career changes for them would be from I.R.S. agent to federal road construction worker. It appears to me that there is an unlimited demand for workers in this field. I swear that you wouldn't even notice another 20 or 30 workers standing around the average construction site. They would blend in; you wouldn't even need to keep them busy.

They could solve the problem of excess dog waste on our city streets by being strategically placed as fire hydrant

82

shields. They could then be called: "Objectionable Materials Interceptors".

$$$

Another position where they would be right at home with a minimum of re-training is that of postal employee. A few million extra employees hanging around the post office on break would be perfectly natural. They're already experts at sending bills to the wrong address and by the slowest possible means.

$$$

One more government position which has the potential to easily absorb a few million excess I.R.S. agents is that of Congressional staff person. If you divide 25,000,000 (the approximate number of excess agents) by 500 (the approximate number of Congress Persons and Senators), you get a mere 50,000. That's the number of extra staff people each congressional representative would have to hire in order to keep all of these people employed. That many should be a snap to keep busy working on re-election campaigns alone, let alone doing background research on prospective opponents, or lobbying for the interests of government employees.

$$\$\$\$$

With their awareness of human needs, alertness, and familiarity with the criminal mind, they would function superbly as prison guards. Their title could be: "Supervisor of Organizational Behavior, Correctional Division".

$$\$\$\$$

Also, because of their special training, they would do well as probation officers for the most dangerous and dysfunctional parolees

One can certainly envision his I.R.S. agent as a junior high P.E. or shop teacher. A good title here could be: "Professor of

84

Hormonal Stress Management".

$$$

It's not hard to imagine him or her as a drivers-ed. instructor either.

$$$

They would make highly effective drug undercover agents in law enforcement.

$$$

They could be used by the department of social services to collect alimony, or for that matter, insurance premiums, in the inner cities.

$$$

They could go to work immediately out in the field soliciting customers for the various welfare programs. Business is good, but imagine how much better it could be with 25,000,000 people out selling those programs.

They could save many lives if they were given flashlights and approved to be used by the Department of Transportation as guard rails on dangerous mountain curves.

$$$

Another practical use for them would be as weather balloons. I'm sure that with enough air pressure, and if all of their leaky openings were sealed closed, sufficient helium could be forced into them to send them to the highest levels of our atmosphere. And they would probably truly enjoy the view from up there.

CATEGORY 2.
MILITARY USES

$$$$$$$$$$$$$$$$$$$$$$$$

They can be used as bumpers on tug boats in place of old tires. Their job title could even be changed to: "Chief Maritime Navigational Aide"

Many of them would function professionally as guard-dogs around the various military installations.

$$$

Agents could march ahead of expensive military hardware such as tanks in order to test for land mines. Their title could be "Explosives and Ballistics Detonation Specialist".

$$$

In a time when so many animals are so badly mis-treated or even in danger of becoming extinct, it would make sense to substitute many of the commonly exploited animals that we have become so accustomed to with former agents of the I.R.S. A good place to start would be to replace all of the parrots aboard naval ships with brightly dressed agents who had mastered sufficient sailor's vocabulary to fill that entertaining role.

And how about the old Dalmatian at the fire station. Why couldn't he be replaced by an agent who could curl up on the rug?

$$$

For that matter, former agents could be used to replaced the over-worked carrier pigeon fleet that carries the over night mail for the post office. Delivery time might even be improved if they were given a bicycle to ride.

Agents could serve as decoys in many dangerous military situations such as being shot into the air with a hot welding torch strapped to their back to decoy enemy heat-seeking missiles. A reasonable title for this job might be: "Director of Military Dis-information".

$$$

Since the average price of an ashtray that the military buys is triple the annual salary of an agent, it seems to me that we could save money by using these guys for small "military" articles such as ash trays. A prestigious job title for this job might be: "Regional Director of Toxic Waste Disposal".

$$$

They would also work as door stops.

(For the same cost-cutting reasons outlined above, they could be used as floor mats.)

(Why not paper weights too?)

They could act as combat photographers since they are accustomed to danger, and they have been trained to follow the orders of superiors without question.

$$$

They could be trained to serve as explosives experts.

CATEGORY 3.
SCIENTIFIC ASSIGNMENTS

$$$$$$$$$$$$$$$$$$$$$$$

An I.R.S. agent would make an ideal tester of new diet products, especially those quick weight-loss programs such as tapeworms, amoebas, and other intestinal parasites. A reasonable title could be: "Federal Eating Disorders Director".

$$$

Agents would be excellent subjects for cosmetic testing in lieu of cute, little, innocent animals like rabbits and hamsters.

$$$

A tremendous economic benefit would occur if we could assign them to donate their extra body organs. Since these cost so many thousands of dollars in a transplant situation, the revenue generated could likely pay their salaries, or the benefits to their heirs for many years.

They make ideal containers for entomologists' maggot collections. We could call them: "Directors of Entomological Research and Control; Larvae Division".

$$$

In areas where volunteers are hard to attract they could be asked to volunteer to test other kinds of products such as snake repellent. Their title could be: "Acting Head of Experimental Deflection".

$$$

In areas of the world where malaria is a problem, they could be used to test new kinds of mosquito repellent.

CATEGORY 4
AGRICULTURAL USES

$$$$$$$$$$$$$$$$$$$$$$$$

Because they are such good conductors, they could be used as poles to

91

connect wires on electric fences.

$$$

Because they are so obnoxious, they make good decoys to keep mad bees off from beekeepers.

$$$

Some of the more athletic former agents would make excellent drags. They can be connected behind tractors in order to level fields. A title could be: "Director of the Federal Bureau of Excavation, Agricultural Division".

$$$

They make fine scarecrows.

$$$

If they could be trained to hold real still, they would work as dams for irrigation.

Their title could be: "Facilitating Director of Hydrological Diversion".

CATEGORY 5
SPORTS AND
ENTERTAINMENT

$$$$$$$$$$$$$$$$$$$$$$$$$

Agents would make good referees in cockfights. We could give them the title of: "Chief of Law Enforcement, Department of Competitive Research".

$$$

They would make good rodeo clowns.

$$$

For particularly difficult and dangerous stunts, where normal people would find the work too dangerous, many would enjoy the excitement of being stunt people.

$$$

They make good bowling pins. They could even set themselves back up after they got knocked down. We could call them: "Recreation Supervisor of Spheroid Reception".

CATEGORY 6
MISCELLANEOUS

$$$$$$$$$$$$$$$$$$$$$$$$

Although not technically within the area of sports and recreation, appliance repair would be a natural for most former agents. They would only have to go to work whenever they feel like it, they could charge exorbitant fees for pretty sloppy work, and they would even have the option of continuing the billing practice pioneered by the I.R.S. of arbitrarily billing anyone whenever they feel like it any amount they can come up with, even if it's not owed.

$$$

The more I think about it though, the more I wonder if perhaps the ultimate occupation for these former I.R.S. agents wouldn't be as a writer. Think about it. You don't have to work if you don't want to; you can say anything you want, even make things up if you don't have anything important to write about; and some idiot will always buy it because the truth was never so entertaining.

12 APPLYING REAL SOLUTIONS

So there you have it, real solutions to real problems. But having this solution actually gain wide approval and be placed into action will take the support of many people on many fronts. The democratic process is slow and expensive in a country the size of ours. If we are to see these proposals become a reality, we must all do our part.

I have also done extensive research, consisting of talking to a couple of people

97

about this topic, and we all agreed that the following things must be done in order to get these changes through Congress:

First: We must immediately begin to break down resistance that will inevitably be thrown up by those who will be asked to change jobs. To do this, we must begin to talk about how prestigious it would be to have the title of "Acting head of the Federal Bureau of Excavation", or "Regional Secretary of De-composition" and other similar new job titles that we have just created.

Second: We must each begin a letter writing campaign today to our individual congress person intimidating them into supporting these changes. The time tested way that you can do this is to make up claims of impropriety and threaten to go public with them if they don't give you what I want. If you are especially convincing, they will often even pay you some of their excess money if you use this strategy. And remember; the more bizarre, outrageous and ridiculous sounding your

98

accusations the better your chances are of making the 10:00 news.

Finally, we must all begin to send large sums of money to me so that I can maintain the installment payments on my tax obligations, provide copies of my returns to the thousands of I.R.S. agents who daily request to see them, while at the same time attempting to placate a small army of creditors (This includes my analyst who incidentally will be happy to vouch for the fact that I am not the least bit paranoid), and other wise keep me out of jail, because, after all, this whole re-assignment thing was my idea. Besides, this job changing program will probably fizzle big-time if I'm not around to head up the new governmental department which will be created and staffed to see it through.

In order to motivate yourself to do your part to carry out this three-pronged attack, I want you to remember back a few years to that Moose convention in Dallas in '84. I was there the whole time with a camera and I have it all on video tape. I also have copies of your tax returns for the past 13 years, and I have been talking to your boss. Don't you be paranoid because I would never consider giving this information to Geraldo unless you force me to.

If this doesn't provide sufficient motivation for you to do your part, imagine, just for a moment, what a wonderful place this country and world will be if we are successful in having these millions of agents of the Internal Revenue Service re-assigned to much more useful positions. The country will prosper, uncle Fred will have to find something else to complain about, birds will chirp, and I'll get rich. What set of goals could possibly be more worthwhile? And besides, ..."Hey, who are you guys?" "Who let you in?" "Don't take my furniture!" "The check is in the mail." "What are you doing to me?" "I know my rights!" "I get one free phone call!" "I'm appealing your decision..." "AAAAAAAHHHHHHH!!!"